DISCOVERING AMERICA
★ An Exceptional Nation ★

American and National Identity

Kristin Thiel

Cavendish
Square

New York

Published in 2019 by Cavendish Square Publishing, LLC
243 5th Avenue, Suite 136, New York, NY 10016

Copyright © 2019 by Cavendish Square Publishing, LLC

First Edition

Cataloging-in-Publication Data

Names: Thiel, Kristin.
Title: American and national identity / Kristin Thiel.
Description: New York : Cavendish Square, 2019. |
Series: Discovering America | Includes glossary and index.
Identifiers: ISBN 9781502643070 (pbk.) | ISBN 9781502642639 (library bound) |
ISBN 9781502643087 (ebook)
Subjects: LCSH: National characteristics, American--Juvenile literature. |
Emblems, National--United States--Juvenile literature. |
United States--Civilization--Juvenile literature.
Classification: LCC E169.1 T47 2019 | DDC 973--dc23

Editorial Director: David McNamara
Editor: Caitlyn Miller
Copy Editor: Rebecca Rohan
Associate Art Director: Alan Sliwinski
Designer: Joe Parenteau
Production Coordinator: Karol Szymczuk
Photo Research: J8 Media

The photographs in this book are used by permission and through the courtesy of: Cover, Moodboard/Brand X Pictures/Getty Images;
Background image of grass and sky TK pp. 20, 21, 26, 27, 40, 41, 46, 47, 62, 68, 69, 78, 79, 86; p. 4 © North Wind Picture Archives; p. 7
Peter V. Bianchi/National Geographic/Getty Images; pp. 11, 15, 46 MPI/Archive Photos/Getty Images; p. 14 Harold M. Lambert/Kean
Collection/Archive Photos/Getty Images; p. 17 Benjamin Franklin (1706–1790)Library of Congress/File: Benjamin Franklin - Join or
Die.jpg/Wikimedia Commons/Public Domain; p. 20 Joseph Sohm/Shutterstock.com; p. 27 http://www1.nyc.gov/site/designcommission/
publicprograms/cityhall/portraits/portrait.page?portraitId=37/File: Hamilton Trumbull - 1805.jpg/Wikimedia Commons/Public
Domain; p. 28 Delpixel/Shutterstock.com; p. 31 Universal History Archive/UIG/Getty Images; p. 34 NavSource Online: Service
Ship Photo Archive (http://www.navsource.org/archives/09/46/46021c.htm)/File: Constitution1803.jpg/Wikimedia Commons/Public
Domain; pp. 37, 60, 61 Bettmann/Getty Images; p. 41 The LIFE Picture Collection/Getty Images; p. 44 Alexander Gardner (1821–1882)
Library of Congress/File: PinkLinkMc alternate.jpg/Wikimedia Commons/Public Domain; p. 49 Engraved by J.C. Buttre from a
daguerreotype/File: Frederick Douglass as a younger man.jpg/Wikimedia Commons/Public Domain; p. 50 PhotosbyAndy/Shutterstock.
com; p. 55 unattributed; based on the depiction from a mechanical glass slide by T. M. McAllister of New York, ca 1865-75/Heritage
Auctions/File: Lincoln assassination slide c1900.png/Wikimedia Commons/Public Domain; p. 58 John N. Choate/Archive Photos/Getty
Images; p. 67 Gift, Ansel Adams, 1902-1984, Library of Congress; (Public Domain) p. 72 Ariel Skelley/DigitalVision/Getty Images;
p. 75 George Lacks/The LIFE Picture Collection/Getty Images; p. 77 Kamira/Shutterstock.com; p. 81 Warren K. Leffler/U.S. News &
World Report Collection (https://memory.loc.gov/ammem/awhhtml/awpnp6/usnews_coll.html) Library of Congress/File: Civil rights
march on washington dc schools.tif /Wikimedia Commons/No Copyright Restrictions; p. 85 InSapphoWeTrust (https://www.flickr.
com/people/56619626@N05)Los Angeles, CA/File: Stonewall Inn, West Village (6445657017).jpg/Wikimedia Commons/CCA-SA
2.0 Generic; p. 88 Encyclopaedia Britannica/Universal Images Group/Getty Images; p. 93 LightField Studios/Shutterstock.com.

Printed in the United States of America

★ CONTENTS ★

People cheer a 1776 reading of the Declaration of Independence.

Chapter One

Identity in the Beginning: 1491 to 1800

★ ★ ★ ★ ★ ★ ★

National identity is a complicated matter. For example, there are two perspectives on what it means to be an American: how an American understands what it means, and what others in the world think it means to be a person from the United States. Everyone has their own perspective on what it means to be from any given nation. Americans debate among themselves about the definition of identity. Even these debated definitions change over time as outside influences affect people. Over the relatively short, but dense, history of the United States, questions of identity have shaped policy, ideas about freedom and democracy, and people's very lives.

★ ★ ★ ★ ★ ★ ★

The First Americans

In the late 1400s, the United States did not yet exist. At that time, the land was alive with established communities, and the area's first immigrants, the Europeans, were soon to arrive. The 1400s is an important time in discussions of American identity for two main reasons. First, the Native peoples who thrived then are known today as the first Americans, Native Americans. Therefore, in discussing American identity, we must discuss Native cultures. Second, white European settlers' general interactions with Native groups established definitions of identity then and established identity issues that continue today. The settlers' systematic destruction of these groups—first through disease and then through war, forced displacement, and discriminatory laws—was supported by racism. American identity is full of positives, and celebrating one's race and ethnicity as well as others' heritages can be positive. The country is known around the world for being a melting pot where people share a common national identity that isn't based in a common ethnic heritage. However, the interactions between colonists and Native peoples demonstrate the first time racism also became a part of the country's identity, something that is part of this identity still.

The year 1492 is often cited as the start of European influence on the Americas. Christopher Columbus landed

The Native Americans of Mesa Verde, in Colorado, were skilled farmers.

in the Bahamas that year, and European invasion and colonization of the Western Hemisphere only sped up after that. However, the land that would become the United States was bustling with complex societies before those European ships landed.

It has been estimated that in 1491, the human population in North and South America combined was more than fifty million—greater than the population of Europe. Ten million people lived in what would become the United States.

Today's anthropologists and geographers identify these large and diverse groups by "culture areas," people with similar languages and ways of living. We often use these same characteristics to self-identify as part of a group, such as a nation. When asked now what makes them a part of a country, and others not members of that country, people will often list having a common language and social norms as important.

The First American Identities

The earliest British settlers would have most regularly encountered the tribes of a couple of culture groups. The members of the Northeast culture area all spoke languages within two linguistic families: Iroquoian and Algonquian. The Cayuga, Oneida, Erie, Onondaga, Seneca, and Tuscarora peoples spoke different but related Iroquoian languages. They lived in villages along rivers and lakes from Canada to North Carolina. The Pequot, Fox, Shawnee, Wampanoag, Delaware, and Menominee peoples spoke Algonquian languages and farmed and fished along the ocean in the same north-south stretch of land.

The members of the Southeast culture area, which ran from the Carolinas to the Gulf of Mexico, all spoke Muskogean languages, farmed, and lived in hamlets. They organized these villages based on social ceremonies and farmers' markets.

The Plains, Southwest, Great Basin, Northwest Coast, California, Arctic and Subarctic, and Southern Plateau culture areas, as well as Hawaii, were all inhabited by people from a diversity of culture and language identities. Some farmed independently; some had sophisticated leadership and social structures. Some lived in adobe villages called pueblos, and some lived in hogans, round houses made of mud and bark.

That is a quick summary of the original human inhabitants of what would become the United States. The people themselves strongly identified with their own communities. For example, in the Northeast, Iroquoian groups were known to form political and military alliances with each other—and to occasionally attack groups outside those confederacies. Or consider the way Native peoples made communal changes after European contact. With the renewed influence of horses on the continent, the Great Plains groups became much more nomadic and started to hunt buffalo across the prairie. "Mission Indians" moved together from the Southwest to California because of colonization by Spaniards. Colonial skirmishes also forced Northeast Iroquois Algonquian neighbors to choose sides.

In the century between when Europeans first reached the "New World" and Virginia was established as the first colony, the Native peoples maintained their homes and community structures. They would trade with Europeans who set up temporary camps and then let the visitors know they needed to move on, until it was time for another trade. This came to an end in large part because of disease. The Native peoples were not immune to the diseases Europeans carried with them, and many died. The colonists established permanent homes, the thirteen colonies, in what appeared to be deserted villages but which were, in essence, graveyards.

The First American Immigrants

England during the 1500s was a land of both great despair and great promise. Because of the demand for wool, farmers converted their land from fields of crops to sheep pastures. This meant workers lost jobs. It also meant food was in shorter supply. Many people could not pay their bills and were going hungry. At the same time, mercantilism was becoming the leading economic theory in Europe. Colonization helped countries practice mercantilism. The more colonies a country had in various places around the world, the greater the diversity of goods the country possessed. Diversification was considered an important goal to meet.

The Identities of the First American Immigrants

The Virginia Company of London started and owned Virginia, the first of the thirteen colonies. Because of this, it had a financial interest in the colonists succeeding.

Specifically, it as well as its shareholders had an economic reason to care. The company sold shares of the colony to wealthy British men. Everyone who bought a share owned a tiny piece of the colony and would receive a portion of the profits the colonists made for the company.

The coat of arms of the Virginia Company of London. The company owned the Virginia colony and was therefore invested in the colonists' success.

The 144 men and boys who sailed on three ships from England in December 1606 and arrived in Virginia in May 1607 shared an identity around labor, commerce, and the single-minded desire for profit. In theory, that was what unified them. In reality, for almost a decade, the founding residents of Virginia were near starvation as they searched for gold, their first idea to make money. They were united in matters of basic survival. They remained employees too, however. In 1609, governmental control even transferred from the British king, James I, to the Virginia Company's investors. They chose among themselves a governor to lead the colonists.

With increasing power over the colony, the company felt its failures even more. The colonists continued to struggle to develop profitable work. This worried investors. The company did not pay out shares of profits, and some investors took the Virginia Company to court. The company decided to try a new public relations angle: it asked people to invest in the colony not for immediate profit but for national pride. They were all British, and Great Britain deserved to be a mighty superpower on both sides of the Atlantic Ocean. If the people supported the Virginia colony—and therefore the Virginia Company—the standard of living would increase as people found jobs and sent the wealth home. This national identity also included racial and religious identities. The company advertised that the colonists would be converting the "godless" Native peoples to the official religion of the British people, the Church of England.

Finally, in 1616, the Virginia colonists figured out they could grow a profitable resource: tobacco. In 1632, a new colony, named Maryland, followed in Virginia's agricultural footsteps. The colonies were dubbed the tobacco colonies. They offer a prime example of how colonies were business opportunities—for England, if not the colonists themselves.

The Southern colonies were also farmland and were used to grow and raise corn, rice, beef, pork, indigo (a plant that created blue dye, good for coloring fabric), and lumber. South Carolina, for example, was owned by whites—first the French for a short time, then the Spanish for a slightly longer time, and finally the British in 1663—but developed and made profitable by slaves. In fact, most of South Carolina's first colonists did not come directly from Britain but from Barbados, a Caribbean colony. Barbados was composed of privately owned plantations worked by slaves. The newcomers brought that system to South Carolina. The slave populations quickly doubled the free white population. The colony also exported slaves to other colonies: these were Native peoples.

The spread of the white population was ethnically motivated. Germans and Scotch-Irish did not want to live near the English, so they settled inland. They felt bonded by heritage against their Native neighbors, so they identified heavily with their isolated communities. They had big celebrations and meals together. Their quilt-making competitions led to quilts being a lasting cultural representation of American identity.

The first New England colonists were the Pilgrims, who landed at Plymouth, Massachusetts, in 1620. They sought religious freedom to practice their puritanical beliefs. Ten years later, Massachusetts became a true business venture when the Massachusetts Bay Company sent many more people across the Atlantic from England to America. Over time, Massachusetts colonists divided along social and religious lines. Those who identified as more conservative formed Connecticut. Those who sought

The passengers of the *Mayflower* landed at Plymouth, Massachusetts, in 1620. They came to the New World in search of religious freedom.

fewer social and religious restrictions formed Rhode Island. Others struck out for New Hampshire.

The middle colonies of New York and Pennsylvania were diverse and prosperous from the beginning. The English were not the first European settlers in what is now New York State. Just as no European cared about pushing Native peoples out, no English colonist cared about overriding the Dutch, Belgian Flemings and Walloons, French Huguenots, Scandinavians, and Germans living in Holland-controlled New Netherland. The English overtook the colony, and they renamed New Netherland as New York in 1664.

In 1680, the king of England added to the large land holdings of William Penn, the founder of Pennsylvania. There, the Quakers' promise of religious tolerance and Pennsylvania's quality soil attracted wealthy people to move from England, seeking new freedoms and work.

The First "Us" Versus "Them" Battles

The divides between Native peoples and European colonists were always apparent and often violent. The American-Indian wars of the 1600s all but destroyed several Native nations. For example, in one year, 1675–1676, the New England Confederation, a militia from parts of what is now the Northeastern United States, committed genocide against the Narragansett, Wampanoag, and Nipmuck

Native Americans and colonists fought in New England during what some called King Philip's War, 1675–1676.

peoples. This was not just about power but about wiping out "the other." Even children were killed.

Pre-Revolutionary Identities

Though today we think of the thirteen colonies as a unit, for most of their existence, they operated independently, claiming their own identities. The Albany Plan of 1754 was the first attempt that came anywhere close to uniting the colonies, and it failed.

The plan came out of the Albany Congress. The British government had ordered the individual colonial governments to meet to draw up a treaty between the British colonists and the Iroquois Confederation of Native peoples. Many colony leaders saw this also as an opportunity to establish a relationship among themselves to help protect each other during the French and Indian War (1754–1763). This conflict was also called the Seven Years' War and occurred as France expanded its land claim and threatened British claims, notably, Virginia. Winston Churchill, who famously led Great Britain during World War II, once said that he considered the French and Indian War the actual first world war.

Benjamin Franklin was one of the colonial leaders who encouraged the thirteen colonies to come together in preparation for war. His newspaper, the *Pennsylvania Gazette*, published the now famous cartoon "Join or Die."

It showed how, alone, the colonies were just pieces of a cut-up, and therefore dead, snake. Together, however, they would be whole, strong, able to strike—they would be alive.

Only seven colonies sent representatives to the Albany Congress. They were Maryland, Pennsylvania, New York, Connecticut, Rhode Island, Massachusetts, and New Hampshire. The representatives saw the Albany Plan not as an act of resistance against the British government but as an acknowledgment that the colonies shared common interests. Though those representatives agreed that the colonies should come together, no colonial leader followed through.

The Treaty of Paris of 1763 ended the French and Indian War but launched the thirteen colonies' revolt

Benjamin Franklin's political cartoon urged the colonies to unite as one.

against Great Britain. Though Britain won the war against France, it accrued a lot of debt during the years of fighting. To make some money, and to tighten its control over the American colonies, it started trying to collect more taxes. The Stamp Act of 1765 taxed newspapers, college diplomas, and most legal documents and licenses. Nine colonial governments registered official complaints, and people throughout the colonies refused to pay the tax. By the time of the Boston Tea Party in 1773, which was the colonists' revolt against increased import taxes, tension between the two groups was incredibly high.

The British government's four Coercive Acts were meant to punish the colonists for the Boston Tea Party. They also shined a light on the division in identity between the two groups. The Boston Port Act said "they," the colonists, had to pay "us," the British, for the ruined tea, and until they did, the British would keep the port of Boston closed. The Massachusetts Act restricted democratic town meetings in the colony. The Administration of Justice Act put British officials above the law in Massachusetts—they could do as they wished without fear of being prosecuted. The Quartering Act forced colonists to house British troops at their own expense. In this way, geography became a part of identity: people in the colonies faced different demands and were held to a different standard than people who lived in Great Britain.

A fifth act from the same time as the four Coercive Acts was called the Quebec Act. It added another layer to the identity question. Many colonists called the five acts together the Intolerable Acts. Protecting freedom of worship for Catholics in Canada, which the Quebec Act did, sounded as horrible, or intolerable, to the Protestant colonists as the invasive punishment of the Coercive Acts did.

The British government hoped that these acts would destroy any cross-colony identity that was forming. The government assumed that by targeting Boston, it could isolate that city, the rest of Massachusetts, and maybe even New England from the rest of the colonies. Instead, the other colonies sided with their neighbor. In September 1774, the First Continental Congress met, in Philadelphia. Unlike the Albany Congress, this meeting was meant to unify colonial resistance to British rule—and it succeeded in doing so.

Revolutionary Identities

During the American Revolution, colonists identified in one of two major ways: they were either Loyalists or Patriots.

Loyalists

Loyalists were also called Tories. They sided with, or were loyal to, Great Britain. They did not form one Loyalist military. Instead, individuals either joined the British army or formed their own support units.

About one-third of the colonists were Loyalists. No one geographic, economic, or religious group was fully Loyalist, but some groups tended to have more Loyalist members than others.

Most lived in New York and many in Pennsylvania and the Southern colonies, though they were not the majority in any of those places.

Many Loyalists had something to gain if Great Britain remained in charge. Some owned a lot of land or were wealthy merchants who feared that war would destroy their property or threaten their businesses. Of course, those individuals who worked for the British government or the Anglican church also wanted to remain loyal. Some, like Quakers, were pacifists, so they rejected war, which meant they had to continue to accept British rule.

After the British army was defeated and the United States became an independent country, people continued to view Loyalists as separate from the mainstream. The new US Congress recommended punishing those who had identified as Loyalists, and all state governments followed this recommendation. For example, people who had identified as Loyalists were usually forbidden from holding elected political office and their property was either taken from them or heavily taxed.

American and National Identity

Eventually, Americans' interest in punishing those who had remained loyal to Britain lessened. William Johnson of Connecticut had been a Loyalist, but he was accepted as part of the Constitutional Convention. By the early 1800s, all laws against Loyalist families had been repealed.

Patriots

Patriots, a term popularized by Benjamin Franklin, supported independence from Britain. They were the majority of colonists. They demonstrated their support by turning out in force at the beginning of the war. Thousands of individuals, carrying their own personal guns, arrived in Concord, Massachusetts, in time for what would become the first day of war: April 19, 1775. By the next morning, twelve regiments had assembled from Massachusetts. Connecticut sent one-quarter of its males who were of fighting age. By June, the Continental Army, the future country's first national military, had been formed.

Though today we think of Patriots as people born in the colonies and fighting for their independence, their true identity is more complex. The first wave of troops were free, property-owning troops fighting for national freedom. As the war dragged on, more and more of those people realized how much they could lose—from their livelihoods to their lives—if they kept fighting. Fewer and fewer volunteered to join or to continue fighting. Two

A Document of Identity

The Constitution of the United States established the new country's government, its foundational laws, and its citizens' basic rights. Many people consider it a major part of the American identity. The United States is not a nation built on one shared race or religion, for example. Americans' common trait is agreeing to live by the rules set forth in the Constitution.

The National Archives' website features a transcript of the Constitution.

The Constitution begins:

We the People of the United States, in Order to form a more perfect Union, establish Justice, insure domestic Tranquility, provide for the common defence, promote the general Welfare, and secure the Blessings of Liberty to ourselves and our Posterity, do ordain and establish this Constitution for the United States of America.

Delegates to the Constitutional Convention in Philadelphia signed the Constitution on September 17, 1787. Like many of the senators and representatives throughout the history of the United States, the fifty-five delegates from twelve of the thirteen states had a shared identity. They were well educated and had careers; many had served in the military, and some had political experience; most were Protestants and in their thirties and forties. All were white males.

Because the Constitution enshrines the fundamental ideas behind what makes the United States a country, many see it as key to the American identity. The centuries-old document is referenced regularly in twenty-first-century news as people debate modern issues such as gun rights and safety and freedom of religion—issues that are themselves tied up in identity.

years after the war started, there was a need for a draft. By April 1777, Congress recommended that states force men to serve in the military. By 1778, the Northern colonies were enlisting African Americans.

General George Washington had forbidden black men from fighting for two main reasons. As a slave owner himself, he feared that arming African Americans could lead to a slave rebellion. Also, many white soldiers did not want to fight alongside people they considered inferior. Overall, 5 percent of the total number of men who served in the Continental Army were African Americans.

The military also started paying mercenary soldiers. Therefore, after 1777, the average Patriot was young, single, incredibly poor, and often a new immigrant. Most of the Continental Army for most of the war was fighting against a ruler they did not even identify as being their ruler.

Because of the brutal battles between the Native peoples and the colonists, when the American War for Independence started, most Native peoples east of the Mississippi River sided with the British military. This encouraged the colonists to turn against the Native nations even more. Again, the divide was ultimately one of identity. The British supported Native resistance groups as long as it benefited them. As soon as they could make peace with other European groups, they dropped their Native allies. The Treaty of Paris of 1783 ended the Revolutionary War, established the borders of the United States, and recognized American independence. It did not acknowledge the nations of Native people at all and gave away land they had lived on for much longer than the European settlers had. These Native peoples were not considered Americans. Until the Indian Citizenship Act of 1924, almost 150 years later, citizenship for Native peoples was extremely limited.

The End of the Revolutionary War

On September 28, 1781, George Washington, serving as commander of seventeen thousand French and American troops, began attacking nine thousand British soldiers at Yorktown in Virginia. The Battle of Yorktown raged nonstop until October 17, when Charles Cornwallis surrendered his British troops. That would be the last battle of the Revolutionary War. Peace talks began.

Throughout the war, matters of identity were always at the forefront. People did feel British or anti-British. Some people considered themselves patriots, but with a lowercase "p"—they felt a part of this "new" land, but they did not want revolution. Political partisanship also mattered, often above all else. People who identified as Whigs tended to side with the revolutionaries. Even after the war, they claimed that their Whig identity put them in a higher position of power than their fellow Americans who had been Tories, regardless of their feelings about the war.

Alexander Hamilton was one of the thirty-nine delegates who signed the Constitution in 1787. He represented New York State at the Constitutional Convention, though he did not grow up there. In fact, he was born on the Caribbean island of Nevis. His childhood was difficult. His father abandoned the family, and Hamilton had to start working at age eleven. Not long after that, his mother died. However, Hamilton also had a lot going for him: he was smart, sociable, and ambitious, and he knew some good people. When he was a teenager, his bosses paid to send him to school in New Jersey. Hamilton went on to study at what would become Columbia University in New York.

Hamilton's life story is bound up in matters of American identity. He was an immigrant in a country built by immigrants. He was also a Federalist who believed in a strong national government to unite the individual states. Though Hamilton traveled to the Constitutional Convention as a New Yorker, he signed the Constitution as an individual. The other two New York delegates disagreed with the document's Federalist position and wanted greater states' rights.

The popular *Hamilton* musical by Lin-Manuel Miranda is about Hamilton's life and adds layers to the discussion of the United States' founders and identity. The playwright

Artist John Trumbull painted this image of Alexander Hamilton in 1805, the year after the Founding Father died.

is Latino American, the cast is racially diverse (and not primarily white), and much of the music is hip-hop. *Hamilton*, which debuted in 2015, asks its audiences to think a lot about American identity.

George Washington was commander in chief of the Continental Army during the American Revolutionary War and the United States' first president. His farewell address offered advice for the fledgling nation.

Chapter Two

Forming Identities in the New Nation: 1800 to 1877

★ ★ ★ ★ ★ ★ ★

At the turn of the nineteenth century, the United States was facing a new era all its own. Its first president decided not to run for a third term. In his thirty-two-page farewell address to the country in 1796, George Washington had a lot to say about American and national identity. He did not look back at his accomplishments leading a brand-new country. He used the speech to continue to advise the young country as its citizens moved forward.

Washington suggested that the United States would succeed if Americans did not divide along political party or geographic lines and if they stuck together as one, separate from other nations. For decades, his speech was reprinted more often than the Declaration of Independence was. And

★ ★ ★ ★ ★ ★ ★

for a few years, thanks to the War of 1812, the country lived by Washington's words.

The War of 1812: An Often Forgotten Source of American Identity

The War of 1812 has been called a forgotten war. Yet for those who lived it, it was a time of national pride and self-confidence. It ushered in the Era of Good Feelings, a national mood that strengthened a unified identity. This wave of Americanism, of people feeling together as "us," requires a "them." In this case, the "other" was again the British. The War of 1812 was also a turning point in relations between Native people and white settlers.

The Revolutionary War ... Again

The War of 1812 is sometimes called a second American war for independence from Great Britain or even a continuation of the Revolutionary War. As they were during colonial times, Britain and France were still enemies in the 1800s. Both countries recognized the young United States as a potential new resource for the other country. To prevent the United States from directly or indirectly helping France, Britain started treating the United States as though it were still under its control. The United States Congress, led by

The War of 1812 ended with the Battle of New Orleans in 1815.

Henry Clay from Kentucky and John C. Calhoun from South Carolina, ended up declaring war on Great Britain.

Britain did not intend to provoke the United States into war. Rather, to deter an American-French alliance, Britain interfered in American affairs on the sea, on the land, and in trade. On the sea, the British navy went so far as to practice impressment, forcing sailors aboard US merchant vessels to leave their ships and work for the British.

On American soil, Britain supported Native peoples as white settlers tried to expand the American territory by moving west across the continent. In 1811, the governor of the territory of Indiana led US troops to victory in the Battle of Tippecanoe. The victory destroyed an alliance among Native nations. It also convinced many Native peoples in the Northwest Territory—the land west of Pennsylvania, east of the Mississippi River, and northwest of the Ohio River—that there was only one way to stop the American settlers from continuing to steal land: by accepting help from the British.

In matters of international commerce, Britain passed the Orders in Council in 1807. This law required countries to obtain permission from Britain to trade with France. In 1810, the United States responded by saying that if either France or Britain traded respectfully with Americans, the United States would stop trading with the other country.

War Hawks Versus Federalists

Henry Clay and John C. Calhoun were two prominent members of the War Hawks. This group was made up mostly of young men from the South and the West who were elected to Congress in 1810. They were so angry about Britain's meddling that they urged President James Madison to declare war. They also hoped that if they fought against Britain, the United States could take control of Florida, which was owned by Spain, a British ally.

Americans who identified as Federalists opposed the war. Major political leaders like John Adams and Alexander

Hamilton identified as Federalists. (Washington hated political division, but his political viewpoints also aligned with Federalism.) Still, the Federalist party was the minority party. It almost dissolved when Thomas Jefferson, from the one other political party of the time, the Democratic-Republicans, won the presidency in 1804. However, the War of 1812 encouraged more people to identify as Federalists. In fact, Delaware, Maryland, North Carolina, New York, New Jersey, and all of New England except Vermont voted Federalist. The war caused the country's first major post-independence divide by political party. This divide did not last long. Federalists were labeled as antipatriotic after the war, and the party crumbled.

Symbols of Identity: Old Ironsides

Though the War of 1812 is no longer a commonly referenced part of American history, more than one lasting cultural touchstone came of the conflict. The enduring importance of these symbols demonstrated American unity under one identity. Old Ironsides is one such symbol.

Before it became known as Old Ironsides, the US Navy frigate *Constitution* was just a common warship. It became famous for unexpectedly beating the seemingly superior British navy. Even its escapes seem heroic. The first time it met the enemy during the War of 1812, it was outnumbered. Five British ships surrounded it. The

The USS *Constitution*, or Old Ironsides, is the oldest ship in the US Navy. It became famous in the War of 1812.

Constitution captain and crew knew that the only way they would survive would be if they escaped. Then the wind died. All the warships, American and British, were powered by wind. The *Constitution*'s crew had to think of a creative solution. For thirty-six hours, until the wind started blowing again, they stayed just out of reach of the British by using rowboats to tow the frigate. They also tossed the *Constitution*'s anchor ahead and then reeled it in, which pulled the warship forward.

American and National Identity

The second time the *Constitution* met the enemy, a battle was possible—the British warship *Guerrière* was alone in the Atlantic Ocean between Nova Scotia, Canada, and Boston, Massachusetts. During the fighting, the *Constitution* seemed immune to the British weapons. Witnesses reported that the cannonballs seemed to bounce off the ship's sides like they were made of iron rather than wood. Though the wooden ship was of course damaged, its crew did win that battle. The myth around this win earned the ship its nickname, Old Ironsides.

The ship's many successes united the American public behind the war effort. In 1830, the US Navy considered taking Old Ironsides apart and using its pieces as scrap. The American public protested. They did not want this American symbol destroyed. To this day, the *Constitution* is a featured destination on Boston's Freedom Trail. Docked at Charlestown Navy Yard, it can be toured almost every day of the year.

Symbols of Identity: "The Star-Spangled Banner"

British forces captured Washington, DC, on August 24, 1814. They burned the Capitol and the White House. Three weeks later, a twenty-five-hour British attack on Fort McHenry in Baltimore inspired the creation of what would become a major symbol of American identity: the national anthem.

Maryland-born lawyer Francis Scott Key was in the middle of meetings on a ship anchored in Baltimore's harbor when the Fort McHenry battle started. He became emotional when he saw American troops finally raise a giant US flag in victory over the fort. He immediately wrote the first verse of a poem and called it "The Star-Spangled Banner." The American flag, or banner, with its "broad stripes and bright stars," had been a meaningful visual to Key. Newspapers across the East Coast published his poem.

Then, after the Civil War, Americans were desperate for unity. They appreciated the image of the "star-spangled banner" waving "o'er the land of the free and the home of the brave," as Key had described. In 1916, President Woodrow Wilson signed an executive order stating that the song was the national anthem. In 1931, Congress made Wilson's declaration official.

From then on, "The Star-Spangled Banner" has also been tied to national identity. It is considered part of patriotic ritual, uniting all who sing it. When Americans choose not to sing, some people view this as displaying an identity that is anti-American. Others say that protest built this country and that speaking up for positive change could lead to a more successful country with more people feeling included in the American identity.

Francis Scott Key was inspired by an early American symbol: the flag. Key wrote a poem that later became "The Star-Spangled Banner."

Identity after War

The War of 1812 reinforced Anglophobia—opposition to, dislike of, and fear of Great Britain—among the American people. It also strengthened patriotism, and being devoted to their country helped people want to identify as Americans. Finally, with the end of the war came the end of Britain's alliance with Native peoples. They would now be more vulnerable to the westward expansion of white settlers. Even the language of identity changed as a result of the War of 1812. After the Revolutionary War, the word "Americans" referred to Native peoples living on the land before white colonists arrived. However, after the War of 1812, the word meant European Americans.

The "Era of Mixed Feelings"

The Era of Good Feelings, a term coined by the Boston newspaper the *Columbian Centinel*, indicated a time when Americans looked inward, happily. From a certain perspective, it felt like the end of the War of 1812 meant Americans could focus on themselves, instead of Europe, and that they could explore developing a new country.

Of course, it is difficult to sustain one national identity in the best of times—and the 1800s were not the easiest of times, for anyone. *Encyclopedia Britannica* calls the period between 1816 and 1850 in the United States "the era of mixed feelings."

The presidential election of 1820 appeared to show unity within the country. With only one political party in the country, James Monroe ran without a major opponent for president in 1820. Unsurprisingly, he won easily. The president's Monroe Doctrine of 1823 appeared to insulate the country further. It said that the United States would not become involved in European situations and would not tolerate European interference in its own. This demonstrated Americans' growing nationalism.

At the same time, people were divided on Supreme Court decisions and expansion into the West, as well as concerned by the Panic of 1819, the country's first financial crisis. Americans were geographically divided, exactly as Washington had warned against.

The Civil War

The biggest divide between Americans was regarding slavery, and that would lead to the Civil War. The issue even divided members of single political parties. Abolitionists wanted the practice stopped completely, or abolished. The Liberty Party was formed wholly as an abolitionist party. The Whigs divided as Conscience Whigs, against slavery spreading to the western territories, and the Cotton Whigs, in favor of as much slave labor as possible.

Members of the former faction helped to form the Free-Soil Party. Those who identified with the free-soil movement depended on the free-labor market to support the growing industrialization in the North and did not want slavery to expand into the western part of the United States. The South's agricultural economy required slave labor to work, Southerners said—and they wanted to expand this practice into the new western territories. Free-soil proponents did not necessarily believe that blacks should be considered equal to whites. Rather, they feared the strong work competition. From 1848 to 1854, the

Lucretia Mott, who was born in 1793 and died in 1880, and Elizabeth Cady Stanton, who lived from 1815 to 1902, organized the Seneca Falls Convention in New York in July 1848. Attendees of this meeting laid the groundwork for women being allowed to vote.

Both women were well educated, unique for women at the time. Mott's family practiced the Quaker religion, which encouraged women to be leaders outside the home. Stanton's father made good money as a lawyer and paid for his daughter to have the level of education he would have offered a son.

Mott did not identify only as a proponent of women's rights; her background as a Quaker guided her to be opposed to slavery. She helped form the Philadelphia Female Anti-Slavery Society in 1833. She was refused entry to the World Anti-Slavery Convention in London in 1840 because she was a woman.

Elizabeth Cady Stanton was also from an abolitionist family. She married an abolitionist, and they spent their honeymoon at the World Anti-Slavery Convention. That was where she and Mott met. Stanton directly linked women's suffrage with African American suffrage, wanting both groups to be granted rights at the same time.

Lucretia Mott was a leading abolitionist and founder of the American women's rights movement.

Free-Soil Party fought against slavery being allowed in the western territories, newly taken from Mexico.

The New York Democrats split with great tension. The Barnburners believed that slavery needed to be destroyed—in other words, if a barn has rats, the answer is to burn the barn down. The Hunker Democrats wanted to maintain the traditional Democratic Party principles, and they were less concerned about slavery. This division was both powerful enough and in a big enough political party that it affected the 1848 presidential election. It may have been a reason Zachary Taylor was elected. He, in turn, surprised people with the way he identified. Though a slaveowner himself, he did not support slavery's expansion. He identified above all else as a nationalist. He was an American, as was everyone around him, and he swore he would keep the country together at any cost.

For everyone, this was another "us" versus "them" identity issue. Henry L. Benning, who would become a general in the Confederate Army, helped encourage his home state of Georgia to secede. He saw African Americans as distinctly different from him and worried that if they were allowed to identify as free, this would affect his own identity. He said: "By the time the North shall have attained the power, the black race will be in a large majority, and then we will have black governors, black legislatures, black juries, black everything. … The consequence will be that our men will be all exterminated or expelled to wander as vagabonds over a hostile Earth."

Lincoln Tries to Keep the Country Together

During his 1860 campaign to become the country's sixteenth president, Abraham Lincoln repeatedly referenced the first president's farewell speech. He wanted everyone to respect Washington's warning about division.

Lincoln won the presidency in 1860, but he did not have the support of the entire country. He won because of the votes of Northerners. He did not receive any electoral votes from the South. As much as this told the new president which citizens liked him and which did not, this told the people that they were divided geographically. Those living in the Southern states no longer had any federal political influence. That's why they chose to secede, an ultimate demonstration of identity. They were no longer Americans but Confederates, members not of the United States but of the Confederate States of America.

The two sides—North and South—used concepts of identity to unite themselves against the other. Northerners labeled Southerners as backward in their thoughts, greedy for power and money, and evil in their treatment of other humans. Southerners likened themselves to rebel groups in Italy, Poland, Mexico, and Greece who had self-identified within their countries.

This photo of President Abraham Lincoln (*center*) was taken not long after the Civil War began.

The World Watches

Newspapers in countries around the world reported on the American Civil War battles. There was an economic reason for their interest—cotton from the slave-supported South was a global commodity, important to industries and merchants around the globe. In fact, the Southern Confederacy attempted to use its important product as currency to get Great Britain and France to help them.

American and National Identity

The two European powerhouses largely did not take the bait, having saved up stores of cotton. But British political cartoonists expressed sympathy for the Confederacy, portraying Abraham Lincoln as the backward leader. (When he was assassinated, their cartoons changed to praise him.)

To people outside the United States, the Civil War also shed a bright light on the fascinating experiment that was the United States. The young country, not even one hundred years old, did not have a national identity based in shared history or even shared religion, culture, or ruling family, as so many other countries did. Instead, the one indisputable thing that bound it was law—its Constitution and system of government. What did that mean when different groups within the country wanted very different things? Southerners called this a fight for self-determination—the right of people who identify together to determine their own future. This was exactly what had led the thirteen colonies to fight for independence from Great Britain. Now, groups identifying in different ways within the country wanted that same opportunity.

Seeking Unity During Division

The year after the Civil War began, people living in Philadelphia asked Congress to celebrate Washington's birthday by reading his farewell address. Philadelphians

People celebrate the ratification of the Thirteenth Amendment, which abolished slavery.

In 1865, the Thirteenth Amendment to the US Constitution abolished slavery in the United States. The Constitution was changed because of the Civil War. President Lincoln believed that emancipating the four million slaves held in fifteen states would help stop the Confederate rebellion in the South and keep the country together.

Under Lincoln's leadership, the Thirteenth Amendment eventually passed in both the Senate and the House of Representatives. The amendment states: "Neither slavery nor involuntary servitude, except as a punishment for crime whereof the party shall have been duly convicted, shall exist within the United States, or any place subject to their jurisdiction."

Though this amendment changed a major document of both American law and identity, in practical ways, there remained stark divisions between those people identified as free and those identified as slaves. For example, immediately after emancipation, black codes were state laws that treated African Americans as less than whites. The country's first civil rights bill, the Civil Rights Act of 1866, passed in response to black codes. In 2016, the documentary *13th* explored how African Americans went from being identified as "slave to criminal with one amendment." The Thirteenth Amendment is part of a racial identity thread that stretches throughout American history.

wanted to remind their fellow citizens of Washington's call for unwavering unity. Lincoln ordered members of the House, Senate, and his cabinet as well as the Supreme Court justices to witness the reading of the address on February 22, 1862, at noon. The Senate continued the annual custom into the twenty-first century.

Approaching Reconstruction

The end of the Civil War, which the North won, did not mean the end of the United States. After such a violent divide, however, the country needed to reconstruct itself. To summarize some of the sentiments around identity at this time, we can turn to the words of Frederick Douglass. Born a slave, Douglass became an international superstar, offering the world his brilliant thoughts regarding slavery.

Before the Civil War, Douglass famously said to an audience of white people on the Fourth of July 1852: "This Fourth of July is *yours*, not *mine*. You may rejoice, I must mourn." He indicated the clear divide that his audience did not want to acknowledge. Even though he was American, because of his race, he was not considered by his society to be American.

As Reconstruction began to reassemble the United States after the Civil War, Douglass wrote, in his 1866 essay "Liberty and Equality for All": The people "want a

Frederick Douglass—leader, intellectual, and activist—published his second autobiography the year of this portrait, 1855.

reconstruction such as will protect loyal men, black and white … This great measure is sought as earnestly by loyal white men as by loyal blacks, and is needed alike by both." He sought to acknowledge a new, and strong, unity of identity. National identity, the Constitution, race—all are bound up in what is "America."

Some Americans identify with this
Robert E. Lee statue in Virginia,
and some want it torn down.

★ Chapter Three ★

Times of Change: 1877 to 1945

★ ★ ★ ★ ★ ★ ★

O n May 7, 1890, a couple hours before sunset, at least
ten thousand people gathered at the James River
port in Richmond, Virginia. Twenty-five years before,
the city had been the Confederacy's capital. Now, those
who gathered used ropes to haul three huge boxes from
a shipping container. They trudged a mile and a half up a
hill to a field that once had grown tobacco but had been
destroyed during the Civil War. There, they opened the
crates and unpacked pieces of a sculpture. Soon, a 60-foot
(18-meter) likeness of Confederate commander Robert E.
Lee atop his horse would "loom over not just the skyline
of Richmond but the psyche of Virginia." This comment
by an article in the *Washington Post*, almost 120 years after

★ ★ ★ ★ ★ ★ ★

the arrival of the Lee statue, talks about the importance of geography, ideology, and symbolism in identity. With the raising of one statue of a Civil War hero, the divide between who was Northern and who was Southern, who was anti-slavery and who was pro-slavery, grew deeper.

The statue made Lee an idol to be admired and followed, even after his death, by white Virginians. Mothers brought their babies so that they could make sure their children, too little to help move the statue, at least touched the ropes. So many more people wanted to help than could fit that they added 700 more feet of rope (213 m) trailing behind the crates, so people could at least hold on to that. Afterward, they cut the rope in pieces for people to keep as mementos. When the assembled statue was revealed on May 29, 1890, there was a parade in celebration. The moment was very much tied to Southern identity.

The Cult of the Lost Cause

The celebrated assembling of Lee's statue began the Cult of the Lost Cause. The Lost Cause was the South's attempt to preserve its "superior" way of life by seceding from the United States. Though it had ultimately failed against its Northern enemy, it did so heroically, said supporters of the Lost Cause idea. To preserve that legacy, they began doing things like erecting memorials to Confederate leaders, naming schools and cities after them, and creating official holidays to the Confederacy.

According to the Southern Poverty Law Center, as of 2015, there were at least 1,503 place names and public symbols dedicated to the Confederacy throughout the United States. Most were created in the first half of the twentieth century, coinciding with Civil War anniversaries and in response to civil rights progress.

Sociologist James W. Loewen has said this is very deliberate propaganda designed to rewrite history. By making the Confederacy appear big and far-reaching, through statues and names, for example, the South appeared powerful despite defeat in the Civil War. For example, Kentucky voted not to secede, yet because of the symbols later placed there, it appears to have always sided with the Confederacy. Kentuckians met Confederate soldiers with animosity, not friendliness. Almost three times as many would fight for the Union as would fight for the Confederacy. In other words, during the Civil War, Kentucky did not identify as part of the South. However, as of 2015, there were seventy-two monuments to the Confederacy and only two to the Union in Kentucky.

Only "fair hands," or white people, pulled the Lee statue up the hill, according to the *Washington Post*. In 1890, John Mitchell, an African American who was also a member of the Richmond city council and editor of a black newspaper, condemned the statue for celebrating Lee's racist and un-American ways. In 2018, Mitch Landrieu, then the mayor of New Orleans, called the Lost Cause propaganda "a lie that distorted history, sought to rationalize lynching, and created a second class of citizenship for African-Americans … send[ing] a specific message to African-Americans" from those who identified as white Americans.

The Compromise of 1877

Of course, African Americans hardly needed statues and other symbols of regional identity to understand that the whites, who were in power, identified them as the "other." The Civil War ended in 1865 with Northern victory and the abolition of slavery, but that did not mean peace and a unified American identity existed. The Reconstruction era, the rebuilding of the two sides of the Civil War into one nation, lasted more than a decade. It was a complicated process with an unsatisfying conclusion in 1877.

The Many Reconstructions

President Lincoln gave a speech on April 11, 1865, that started to talk about ideas for reconstructing the country. Three days later, he was assassinated. His successor, Andrew Johnson, ushered in what would be called Presidential Reconstruction. The South took advantage

John Wilkes Booth assassinated President Abraham Lincoln while Lincoln watched a play in 1865.

of Johnson's lenient plan and continued to treat African Americans as slaves who had no rights, essentially.

This infuriated the North, including the Northern-controlled Congress. Radical Reconstruction followed. During this period, the South was seen not just as the war's loser; Congress also temporarily divided the region into five military districts. By force, progress started to happen. African Americans received rights, and states were made to uphold those rights.

The pendulum swung quickly again, however. White supremacists of the South violently pushed back against the North's demands. This affected the presidential election of 1876 and called Rutherford B. Hayes's win into question.

With the Compromise of 1877, Southern politicians promised to accept Hayes's presidency and respect civil and political rights of all citizens. In return, the North had to withdraw troops from the South, and the South had to be given more political power in the president's cabinet, along with federal funding for their railroad. Without threat of consequences and with new power, the South did not follow through on its promises. Racial equality was short-lived, and the statues to race-based identity, literal and figurative, started to go up.

The Gilded Age

Mark Twain and Charles Dudley Warner's coauthored novel, *The Gilded Age: A Tale of Today*, satirized the greed and corruption of post–Civil War America. Its title was adopted as a common nickname for the era between Reconstruction and the turn of the twentieth century. During this time, American racial and class identity were tied up in immigration and territory expansion and agricultural and industrial development.

New Attempts to Misidentify Native Peoples

Railroad travel changed after the Civil War. Newly invented air brakes allowed trains to stop more dependably. The addition of sleeping and dining cars encouraged people to travel longer distances because trains were more comfortable. This technology went hand in hand with political decisions. The Pacific Railway Acts of 1862 and 1864 helped to build transcontinental railroads. The 1862 Homestead Act allowed all Americans, including freed slaves, to settle on federal land for free. The US federal government wanted people to travel to and settle the West to enlarge the country. This expansionism led to wars for land between whites and Native peoples. At the close of these wars, the Dawes Act of 1887 created what are now known as reservations. The US federal government divided up land for Native peoples to live on. The government hoped the Native people would farm just as the white people did, shedding their old racial and cultural identities for the white people's.

The government also established Indian boarding schools because officials began to think that assimilation was the easiest way of "dealing with" Native peoples. A US Army officer, Richard Pratt, founded the first school. He said his goal with educating each Native person was to "kill the Indian in him, and save the man." Interestingly, only a few decades later, during World Wars I and II, the same

These Chiracahua Apache children were forced into a boarding school in 1886 by order of the US government.

federal government that tried to force Native peoples to "be like white people" was welcoming their unique identity. The government hired the Choctaw in World War I and the Navajo in World War II to be code talkers, using their complex languages to communicate secret tactical messages the enemy could not crack.

Immigrants Versus Immigrants

As concerned as many American-born whites were about African Americans and Native peoples, they were also concerned about immigrants during the Gilded Age. The

United States' population increased from about forty-nine million in 1880 to seventy-six million in 1900. About 72 percent of these immigrants came from Germany, Great Britain, Ireland, and Scandinavia. Many were Catholic or Jewish, and many were not classified as white, according to the racial definitions of that era. These immigrants formed strong communities in their new country. Once they were settled, they brought family and friends over, who brought more family and friends over. Living near each other in the United States, they spoke their native languages. They found strength in their unity.

About 180,0000 Chinese immigrants arrived in the United States between 1849 and 1882. Many other immigrants and American-born people viewed these Chinese immigrants as an inferior race. A large percent of Americans were also fearful that Chinese immigrants would push them out of jobs. Pressured by their voters, Congress passed acts that prevented immigration from China. Chinese merchants responded by boycotting products from the States, but the boycott lasted only five months.

World War I

After the Gilded Age, one of the next big events that formed America's identity was World War I. After remaining neutral for the war's first three years, the United States sent troops to Europe in 1917. It was the first time the country had gone abroad to help defend another's land. American participation in the war was a turning point. It was when the rest of the world began to view the country as an international superpower. President Woodrow Wilson accepted this identity. For example, he suggested the formation of the League of Nations after the war. The league was designed to foster international relations. Members would work together to resolve disputes between countries before war broke out.

Women's Identities in World War I

Beyond changing perceptions of America internationally, World War I shaped American identities within the country. Individual participation in the war changed perspectives

during and after the war. For example, over the year and a half that the United States was involved in the war, four million men served in the US armed

Many women, such as this one running a lathe that shapes wood and metal, filled jobs while men fought abroad in World War I.

American and National Identity

forces. So many men fighting abroad meant women stepped in to roles that were previously not an option for them. More than sixteen thousand women also went overseas to aid in the war effort. They worked as clerks, telephone operators, and nurses, and ran restaurants for the soldiers.

African American Identities in World War I

For African Americans, there was great debate about whether to fight in the First World War. The famous black writer and activist W. E. B. Du Bois thought that African Americans showing patriotism by serving in the military would lead to new respect and rights back home after the war. James Weldon Johnson, an early civil rights leader, asked why fighting in the war should matter. The African American person, he wrote, "has been here three hundred years; that is, about two hundred years longer than most of the white people."

Those African Americans who did serve had life-changing experiences in Europe. The US military segregated them from

W. E. B Du Bois cofounded the National Association for the Advancement of Colored People (NAACP), an important organization still in operation today.

During the Prohibition era, from the Congressional approval of the Eighteenth Amendment to its repeal in 1933, it was illegal to make, carry, or sell alcohol in the United States. It was not illegal to drink alcohol.

The Eighteenth Amendment to the US Constitution, ratified in 1919, reads: "After one year from the ratification of this article the manufacture, sale, or transportation of intoxicating liquors within, the importation thereof into, or the exportation thereof from the United States and all territory subject to the jurisdiction thereof for beverage purposes is hereby prohibited."

Historians believe Prohibition was not an issue of morality, even though followers of the temperance movement believed that abstaining from drinking would end all social problems.

Bryant Simon, a professor of urban history, described a political cartoon from the time. Wooden barrels of liquor are walking down the street holding protest signs. None talk about morality, Simon said; instead, they talk about how alcohol "creates disorder." Prohibition, Simon explained, was about "reforming the product of industrialized society—workers themselves."

the rest of the units and did not treat them as equal to white units. However, they often received fair treatment from their French allies. Because of this, after the war, they returned to the United States with a clearer perspective on racial inequalities.

The Repeal of Prohibition

The Twenty-First Amendment, ratified in 1933, had a simple mission. It reads: "The eighteenth article of amendment to the Constitution of the United States is hereby repealed." The Noble Experiment, as Prohibition was nicknamed, turned out to be an impressive failure. It caused economic problems and increased crime.

A lot of people lost their jobs when breweries, distilleries, and bars shut down. Unable to make money off drinks, restaurants couldn't make enough money to stay open. Theater revenue plummeted. Individuals, businesses, and industries were not the only ones to suffer; the federal government also lost money. It lost about $11 billion in excise tax revenue, money collected on things like alcohol, while it spent $300 million to enforce the ban on alcohol.

People in support of Prohibition claimed it would lower crime rates. Instead, previously law-abiding people became criminals if they made their own liquor, a practice called bootlegging. Police officers were tempted by bribes to ignore the bootlegging. Professional criminals made a lot of money. For instance, Al Capone made $60 million a year from his bootleg business.

Franklin D. Roosevelt won the presidency in 1932 by running on a platform to end Prohibition. The Eighteenth Amendment became the first amendment to be repealed.

World War II

World War II began when the youngest World War I soldiers were still fit enough to fight—just two decades separated the two wars. Thirty countries took sides in response to Adolf Hitler's Nazi German forces invading Poland in September 1939.

Great Britain and France were the first to declare war against Nazi Germany. The United States maintained an isolationist policy; Americans desired a clear distinction between them and the rest of the world. Their involvement in World War I had been too costly, in terms of human life and resources, and they wanted to steer clear of another war overseas. In fact, in the years between the two world wars, Congress passed federal laws to protect the country against getting involved in another world war. The Neutrality Act of 1935 forbade the United States from sending even nonhuman resources, such as guns, to all sides in a conflict.

However, President Franklin D. Roosevelt appeared to waver in his isolationism. He called Congress into special session to revise the Neutrality Act to sell weapons to Britain and France. This almost lost him the 1940 presidential election. To win, he had to publicly promise the country would not send troops into battle. Back in office, Roosevelt grew his support of the Allied forces, those fighting against the Axis powers of Germany, Italy, and Japan.

It appeared more and more likely that the United States would get involved. An attack by Japan hastened that. The day after Japan attacked the Pearl Harbor naval base in Hawaii, on December 7, 1941, the United States declared war against Japan. On December 11, Germany and Italy declared war against the United States, which then declared war against them.

Approximately forty to fifty million soldiers and civilians died, including at least six million Jews, before Allied victory was declared in 1945. The world changed forever under this gruesome toll. American identities also changed.

Japanese Internment Camps

Executive Order 9066, signed by President Franklin D. Roosevelt on February 19, 1942, forced thousands of issei, Japanese immigrants, and nisei, first-generation Americans born to parents who had immigrated from Japan, out of their homes and into camps. About 117,000 people, most of whom were American citizens, were put in isolated military zones in California, Oregon, and Washington.

They were, according to the order, "subject to whatever restriction the Secretary of War or the appropriate Military Commander may impose in his discretion." This was done in response to the Japanese military bombing Pearl Harbor in Hawaii.

Starting on March 24, 1942, everyone who was at least one-sixteenth Japanese was evacuated. This included both the very young and the very old and those who were sick or had physical disabilities. They had six days to pack what they could carry and relocate to repurposed fairgrounds, racetracks, and animal stalls. In Portland, Oregon, three thousand people stayed in a livestock pavilion leftover from a farm exposition. There were food shortages and sanitation issues in these places. If there was any protest, police and guards would tear-gas the interned people; sometimes, they killed people.

At first, even the Supreme Court upheld the constitutionality of the executive order. They ruled as such in the 1944 case *Korematsu v. United States*. Fred Korematsu, the plaintiff in the case, was a twenty-three-year-old Japanese American citizen who went to great lengths to change his outward identity to avoid internment. He had plastic surgery to change the shape of his eyes so that he could claim to be of Spanish and Hawaiian descent and changed his name. His plan to evade capture worked for a short time, but he was

The Manzanar Relocation Center in California was one of ten internment camps the US government forced Japanese Americans into during World War II.

eventually arrested. The American Civil Liberties Union stepped forward to represent him. The Supreme Court ruled that the executive order was a necessity in the time of war and was not racially motivated.

It took until 1945, and the Supreme Court case *Endo v. the United States*, for the order to be declared unconstitutional. Mitsuye Endo brought the case forward. The government offered to free her if she would drop the case, but Endo refused. She wanted to force her case to be heard in hopes that it would free everyone, not just her.

Rosie the Riveter

World War II had a symbol of working women's new identity: Rosie the Riveter. In 1942, the Westinghouse Electric Corporation hired artist J. Howard Miller to design a poster to help the company recruit workers. Miller's image was of a woman in a red-and-white polka-dot headscarf and blue shirt. She stood flexing her muscles. The poster proclaimed, "We Can Do It!" Westinghouse displayed it for two weeks in February 1943. It was only one of about forty such posters, and it was one of the few that featured women.

The poster did not name her Rosie, but she received that name after a related image was published in the popular *Saturday Evening Post* on May 29, 1943. The magazine published artist Norman Rockwell's painting of a woman in a blue factory uniform with a rivet gun in her lap on its cover. She held a sandwich in one hand, likely taken from her lunch box, which was labeled "Rosie." Under her foot was Adolf Hitler's racist tract *Mein Kampf*. Coincidentally, at the same time, Redd Evans and John Jacob Loeb's song "Rosie the Riveter" became popular. Rosalind P. Walter, who was a riveter on Corsair fighter planes, inspired the Evans and Loeb song. People combined the image with the song in their minds.

Rosie the Riveter has become a recognizable symbol, appearing everywhere from posters to postage stamps.

The image of Rosie was not as well known in the 1940s as she has become. She has, over time, become a symbol of feminist strength. In the 1980s, around the fortieth anniversary of World War II and in the middle of renewed efforts for women's rights, the US National Archives licensed the image. Though she was not considered a major symbol of identity in the 1940s, she is now.

African American Identities in World War II

Some of the identity changes during World War II were positive. For example, labor leader and activist A. Philip Randolph made huge changes for African Americans. He took his first steps in this direction during World War I, when he tried to unionize African American shipyard workers and elevator operators. His Brotherhood of Sleeping Car Porters, founded in 1925, became the first official African American labor union by 1937.

This was just in time for Randolph to turn his attention toward ending racism in the workforce at the federal level. After World War II started, he planned a march on Washington to protest discrimination in industry. If democracy did not offer every American defense, protection, and equality, he said, "it is a hollow mockery and belies the principles for which it is supposed to stand."

President Franklin D. Roosevelt met the activists' demands quickly. He issued an executive order that banned racial discrimination in government defense. It also created the first Fair Employment Practices Committee.

After World War II ended, Randolph pressed again. His League for Nonviolent Civil Disobedience Against Military Segregation succeeded at getting President Harry S. Truman to issue an executive order banning segregation by race in the US military.

Women's Identities in World War II

As women had stepped into new roles during World War I, they did so in World War II as well. Between 1940 and 1945, nearly 37 percent of the American workforce was women; this was a large increase from 27 percent before the war. By the time the war ended, almost one-quarter of married women worked outside the home. As their returning husbands took advantage of the money offered by the GI Bill to pay for college, many of these women continued working. Dual-income households started to gain a foothold in the country. Some industries were majority women. Around 65 percent of the aircraft industry was women. It had been 1 percent before the war.

Americans have celebrated
the Fourth of July since 1777.

★ Chapter Four ★

Constructing Identities Today: 1945 to Present

★ ★ ★ ★ ★ ★ ★

A grand social and political experiment, a world power, a haven and sanctuary to many—for many reasons, the United States has been a fascination in the world since its birth. Some of the most famous observations of American identity are commentaries from visiting citizens of other countries.

It is nearly impossible to discuss what America *is* in modern day without mentioning what a French sociologist thought it *was* in the early 1800s. Alexis de Tocqueville's *Democracy in America*, published in 1835, remains an often-cited text. He chronicled everything from the country's unique geography to its people's beliefs, preferences, passions, and biases—the national identity. He wondered if

★ ★ ★ ★ ★ ★ ★

Americans' common belief system could hold the country's multicultural society together.

In 1922, the British writer G. K. Chesterton published *What I Saw in America*. The book focuses on the unique aspect that makes the United States the United States: America is held together by core beliefs that Americans voluntarily signed on to follow (quite literally, with the Constitution); it was not founded on common ethnicity or cultural heritage, like European countries. We see that in the debates and issues of the twentieth and twenty-first centuries too.

The Cold War

The Cold War between the United States and the Soviet Union began after World War II, in 1945, and did not end until the Soviet Union collapsed in 1991. Over these decades, the two countries fostered their hatred of each other and pitted their citizens against each other. Though they had been on the same side in the world war, they had been reluctant allies. The Americans were concerned about the Soviet Union's communism, which they saw as a threat to a democratic ideal; the Soviets were bothered that the United States did not recognize their country as a world power.

The Red Scare of the late 1940s and early 1950s provides a great example of how divisions of identity formed during

In 1946, the American Federation of Labor, a collection of workers' unions, held an anti-Communism rally.

the Cold War. Americans often called Communists "Reds" because the Soviet flag was red. Americans had to prove they were American enough or risk being considered treasonous Communists. The House Un-American Activities Committee (HUAC) was a committee of the US House of Representatives. Though it began in 1938, it was strongest in the 1940s and 1950s. If HUAC suspected a person was a Communist, the committee subpoenaed the person. The person had to attend a hearing where they were questioned about their political beliefs and how they lived. HUAC also demanded they provide the names

Section one of the Twenty-Second Amendment states:

No person shall be elected to the office of the President more than twice, and no person who has held the office of President, or acted as President, for more than two years of a term to which some other person was elected President shall be elected to the office of the President more than once. But this article shall not apply to any person holding the office of President when this article was proposed by the Congress, and shall not prevent any person who may be holding the office of President, or acting as President, during the term within which this article becomes operative from holding the office of President or acting as President during the remainder of such term.

By passing on running for a third term, the United States' first president, George Washington, set a two-term pattern that most presidents would follow. President Ulysses

Franklin Delano Roosevelt was elected president four times. After his death, presidential term limits were established to protect American democracy.

S. Grant was open to the idea of serving for a third term, and Theodore Roosevelt ran for a third term in 1912 but failed. President Franklin D. Roosevelt succeeded at winning not three presidential elections but four (he died early in his fourth term as president). Concerns voiced by leaders of the opposition party, the Republicans, affected other politicians and the public. Fearing that unlimited terms could threaten democracy, Congress passed this amendment in 1947, and it was ratified by the states in 1951.

of other possible subversives, or people working against the country. People who refused to cooperate could be imprisoned. If they were allowed to go free, they were usually blacklisted in their industry—they lost their jobs, and no one would hire them.

The Cold War, under which Americans had to assume a clear political identity, and the civil rights movement, under which Americans felt divided by racial identities, overlapped. African American Broadway star, lawyer, and civil rights activist Paul Robeson got caught up in the overlap in a personal way. In 1949, he was misquoted as saying African Americans would not side with their fellow Americans against the Soviets. People began calling him "the Kremlin's voice of America," the Kremlin referring to the Soviet government, and "Black Stalin," referring to Soviet leader Joseph Stalin. Most of his US concerts that summer were canceled. At the one that was not, the audience disrupted it with racial attacks against Robeson. Alternatively, W. E. B. Du Bois sided with the Soviets because he felt communism allowed for a society free of racism.

The Civil Rights Movement

Issues of identity were naturally tied up in the civil rights movement of the 1950s and 1960s. Those involved in the movement were determined to secure rights for African Americans that were equal to those of white Americans.

Rosa Parks is considered one of the founders of the movement. In 1955 Alabama, the law was that buses were segregated into seats for African Americans and seats for whites. Parks, a forty-two-year-old African American woman, boarded a Montgomery city bus after work and sat where the law said she should. However, when the section for white Americans filled up, the bus driver asked Parks to give up her seat to a white man. She refused and was arrested.

Parks was secretary of the local chapter of the National Association for the Advancement of Colored People (NAACP). Because of her work with this early civil rights group, she did not want to accept this unjust arrest. She told her story to prominent activists, who bailed her out of jail and set a protest in motion. The Women's Political Council (WPC), the Montgomery Improvement Association (MIA), led by the not-yet-famous Dr. Martin Luther King Jr., and African American ministers promoted a bus boycott. Around 75 percent of Montgomery's bus riders were African American. The groups hoped that such a huge loss of riders, and therefore fares, would force the city to change its laws. African Americans banded together to keep the boycott going for 381 days. The few who had access to private cars organized carpools. Those who drove taxis charged African American passengers a less expensive fare equal to the cost of riding the bus. Community leaders held regular meetings to keep everyone focused and informed—and united as one group demanding justice. More than a year later, a federal court ruled that bus segregation violated the Fourteenth Amendment of the Constitution—the indisputable defining document of America's national identity.

Many white Americans resisted this legal change, sometimes violently, but this was just the beginning of the civil rights movement's fight against the status quo. Teenagers were part of one of the next defining moments. In 1957, Central High School in Little Rock, Arkansas, tried to desegregate. Until the court case *Brown v. Board of Education* in 1954, American schools were legally allowed to practice a "separate but equal" policy. White students went to one school and African American students to another. After that court ruling, schools had to be integrated, students of all races attending classes together, but schools were slow to do this. The Little Rock Nine, nine African American students, attempted to attend the previously all-white Central High School. The white public, with support from the Arkansas National Guard, was so angry about this that President Dwight D. Eisenhower had to send federal troops to protect the nine students.

A quarter of a million people protested during the March on Washington on August 28, 1963.

In many ways, the civil rights movement continues into the twenty-first century, as African Americans experience greater education issues, incarceration levels, and discrimination by police and citizens alike when compared with whites. The civil rights movement had involved protesters of all races, even during the 1960s. For example, the Freedom Riders of 1961 were made up of both African American and white civil rights activists. They rode buses throughout the South to protest the continuing segregation of bus stations: restrooms, restaurants, and other waiting areas were divided by race. The March on

Washington on August 28, 1963, drew a racially diverse crowd of two hundred fifty thousand people. The peaceful march in the nation's capital sought to prove the popularity of civil rights legislation. Dr. King gave his often-quoted "I Have a Dream" speech on that day.

However, unlike whites, African Americans can never voluntarily opt out of situations. That is a difference of both life and identity. In his 1903 book *The Souls of Black Folk*, W. E. B. Du Bois wrote about the "double-consciousness" that all African Americans feel. By this he meant that African Americans self-identify both as they see themselves and as others see them. Because one cannot hide one's skin color and because race is so much a part of identity politics in America, "one ever feels his two-ness," Du Bois wrote. Being both American and African American led to "two unreconciled strivings; two warring ideals in one dark body." In 1968, King spoke of this also, in his speech "A New Sense of Direction." He said that African Americans are both African and American, both the "heirs" of exploitation, slavery, and powerful cultures and rightfully "tied up with the destiny of America."

Some experts, like Marc Morial, president of the National Urban League, credit the civil rights movement with another shift in identity expression: the twenty-first century "reverse Great Migration" of African Americans to

American and National Identity

the South. The league helped African Americans resettle in Northern cities during the Great Migration. Between 1916 and 1970, more than six million African Americans tried to escape discrimination and lack of opportunities by moving from the South, where their families had lived since they had been brought there as slaves. In 1900, nine out of ten African Americans were Southerners; by 1970, less than half were.

In the twenty-first century, the National Urban League is reporting a repopulation of the South by African Americans. Morial told *USA Today* that the Civil Rights Act of 1957 (that allowed prosecution of anyone who prevented a citizen from voting), the Civil Rights Act of 1964 (that guaranteed employment rights and integrated public places), and the Voting Rights Act of 1965 (that banned literacy tests for voters) started to transform the South. Almost as soon as the Great Migration had ended, African Americans started returning to the South. New York State, Illinois, and California once had the country's largest African American population. Now New York, Florida, and Texas do. Some move there because they have always believed they were Southern at heart, even if they weren't born there, because of family ties. Of course, "Southern" also can mean having Confederate ties. The region has not wholly welcomed its new residents. Journalist and Pulitzer Prize winner Isabel Wilkerson told

USA Today she hoped this new migration would modernize the Southern identity.

Gender and Orientation and Identity

In the 1950s and 1960s, gender identity and sexual orientation had to follow strict definitions—in public. In private, of course, people who might later identify as gay, lesbian, bisexual, pansexual, transgender, and queer shared their true selves. Homosexuality was legal in only one state by 1961, Illinois. Punishment in other states ranged from being forced to pay steep fines to being thrown in jail. Socially, those who identified as anything but male or female and straight, or who were perceived as identifying as something "other," were often harassed and discriminated against.

Therefore, LGBTQ people most often made connections with others at bars and clubs. The Stonewall Inn, in New York City, allowed people to be themselves— for a price. It was run by the mob. The mafia extorted money from wealthy customers by threatening to tell their secret to family and friends if they didn't pay, and they charged steep prices for drinks. Still, patrons were willing to pay because most of the time, the police ignored the Stonewall—the mob bribed them to look the other way.

The Stonewall Inn in New York City is now a National Historical Landmark.

Sometimes the police raided the Stonewall anyway, charging guests with "solicitation of homosexual relations" or "nongender-appropriate clothing." The police raid on June 28, 1969, did not go easily like the others had. Patrons were tired of the abuse, and they resisted arrest. More people from the neighborhood joined in the protest. The violence and destruction around the Stonewall lasted until July 1.

The Stonewall Riots encouraged people to openly identify by whatever gender or orientation they were. The first public advocacy group for gay rights, the Gay Liberation Front, started. The first gay pride parade, on June 28, 1970, was a one-year anniversary celebration of

On September 11, 2001, the United States experienced a massive terrorist attack on its own soil. That day, members of al-Qaeda—an Islamic extremist group— hijacked four airplanes and flew three of those planes into the Pentagon in Arlington, Virginia, and the World Trade Center in New York City. Nearly three thousand Americans lost their lives in the attacks.

In the days and weeks following September 11, Americans banded together to give blood, volunteer, and raise money for the victims and the police officers and fire fighters who paid the ultimate price helping others. It was a time of heightened patriotism as the country reeled from the attacks.

Yet not all Americans built on those feelings of community. In 2001, there were 481 hate crimes directed at Muslims in the United States. Perpetrators of those crimes wrongly conflated Islam and terrorism, though the religion of Islam is by nature a peaceful one. Feelings of fear and mistrust have been perpetuated in the decades after the September 11 attacks, demonstrating just how complex ideas about American and national identity are—and how these ideas are forged by major events.

the Stonewall Riots. On June 24, 2016, President Barack Obama designated the Stonewall Inn as a national monument, the first to commemorate LGBTQ history.

Puerto Ricans Are Americans

One American territory demonstrates just how complicated identity politics is. In September 2017, Hurricane Maria devastated parts of the Caribbean. Puerto Rico was one of the hardest hit islands—which means America was one of the hardest hit countries. Many Americans do not realize that Puerto Ricans are US citizens. According a poll that made headlines in late 2017, only 54 percent of Americans know that people born in Puerto Rico are also Americans.

Puerto Rico's US History

Puerto Rico was under Spanish control for centuries, from the moment Christopher Columbus claimed it for Spain in 1493. In 1898, the United States "bought" the island as part of the treaty ending the Spanish-American War.

English was established as the official language, but most Puerto Ricans spoke Spanish. Until 1902, when Puerto Rican resident Isabel González sued for the right to move freely in all US-controlled lands, Puerto Ricans were considered foreign immigrants if they wanted to

Puerto Rico has been a US territory since 1898. It became a US commonwealth in 1952. Puerto Ricans are American citizens.

live in the United States. Full citizenship was granted to Puerto Ricans with the Jones-Shafroth Act of 1917. This happened during World War I, when the United States feared its enemy, Germany, might invade the Caribbean.

Puerto Rico's Nationalist Movement

There has long been a strong nationalist movement in Puerto Rico, though the votes do not always demonstrate that.

Pedro Albizu Campos, a Harvard-educated attorney and activist and World War I American veteran, is considered the founder of the Puerto Rican Independence Movement. His activism to try to ensure rights for Puerto

Ricans led not only to his imprisonment but to the enactment of Law 53 in 1948. It made talk of independence from the United States and celebration of Puerto Rican identity illegal.

Since Albizu Campos's death in 1965, schools, streets, and buildings have been named for him. Doctor Pedro Albizu Campos Puerto Rican High School was founded in the West Town neighborhood of Chicago in 1972. It is an alternative school that has been changing the identity of Puerto Rican students for the better. In 1987, the school had a 90 percent graduation rate; Puerto Rican students in other high schools in the neighborhood had a dropout rate of nearly that much, between 65 and 75 percent.

The school has supported Puerto Rican independence. In June 1983, seventy FBI agents and police stormed the school, look for ties to what it considered terrorist activities. Later, the US Attorney issued an apology. At the school's first permanent location, the exterior walls were painted with portraits of political prisoners from Puerto Rico and the interior walls covered with advocacy posters. It shared space with a Puerto Rican cultural center. The students say that whether or not they support independence, they are glad to learn Spanish as well as English and the Puerto Rican part of American history in their classes.

In June 2017, Puerto Ricans voted that they wanted to start the process to become a state. However, that vote does not necessarily mean that most Puerto Ricans want statehood; only 23 percent of registered voters cast their votes. Therefore, we only know that a majority of that minority group wants Puerto Rico to become a state.

It's All About the Words

Identity in modern America is still a complex issue. Researchers have always found it useful to identify groups of people by language. An example of this can be seen in the culture areas that researchers defined to categorize Native peoples before European contact. Language is also how many Americans in the twenty-first century self-identify.

In 2016, Pew Research Center asked people in fourteen countries how they knew who "belonged" and who was an "outsider" in their country. Only 32 percent of Americans and 21 percent of Canadians told the survey that it is *very* important for a person to be born in their country to identify as part of that country.

Similarly, only 32 percent of Americans said all Americans should practice one religion, specifically, Christianity. National customs and traditions are very important to American identity for fewer than half of Americans (45 percent) and just over half of Canadians (54 percent).

However, when it came to questions of language, the numbers, and people's beliefs, change—a lot. Most people in every country surveyed said it is very important that someone wanting to identify as a member of that country speak the country's dominant language. In Canada, 59 percent believed this to be true; in the United States, 70 percent did.

How Other Identities Factor

Identities related to age and political party guide how people think about national identity. People ages fifty and older were more likely than people ages eighteen to thirty-four to think birthplace very important to national identity. In the United States, 40 percent from that older group thought people should be born in the States to consider themselves American; 21 percent from the younger group believed that. Most older Americans, 55 percent, responded that Americans should share traditions, while most younger Americans, 72 percent, responded in that way.

The Pew Research Center found that "the debate over national identity is a partisan one." In the United States, people who identify as Republicans think one way about factors of American identity, and people who identify as Democrats think another way. In 2017, the Associated Press-NORC Center for Public Affairs Research (AP-NORC) also found an American identity divided by political party identities.

Overall, 45 percent of Americans responding to the Pew study think shared customs are very important to American identity. This is different for people also identifying as Republican; 60 percent of them think this. Of those identifying as Democrat, 38 percent think this. The AP-NORC study found similar numbers: 35 percent of Republicans versus 66 percent of Democrats think it is extremely or very important to American identity that the United States support cultures and values intermingling within its borders.

To the Pew survey, only 32 percent of Americans overall said those considering themselves Americans should practice Christianity. However, 43 percent of Republicans responded with this belief; 29 percent of Democrats did. The AP-NORC study found an even greater partisan division: 64 percent of Republicans, compared with 32 percent of Democrats, said they believe people calling themselves Americans should follow Christianity.

The AP-NORC survey found that one belief about American identity crosses political party lines. On one point, most people from both major American parties agree. Seven out of ten Republicans and seven out of ten Democrats think the United States is losing its national identity. They know members of the other party have different beliefs about and visions for the country.

Considering American and National Identity

This book has tried to shed light on the many ways that Americans have identified over the centuries—as well as the way others have identified Americans and how Americans

Every American citizen and every new immigrant to the nation shapes American identity.

have identified each other. There are throughlines related to race, gender, politics, and symbols. Above all, one of the things that makes the United States unique is that Americans are united not in ethnic or religious identities, as so many countries are, but in political ideology. Historian Philip Gleason wrote, "The universalist ideological character of American nationality meant that it was open to anyone who willed to become an American."

G. K. Chesterton phrased it more poetically. "In America," Chesterton wrote in *What I Saw in America*, "there are no moods, or there is only one mood … hustle or uplift." Of course, that is but one part of the American identity. The American Chesterton Society said that the creed that Chesterton recognized as uniquely American "remains the ideal that most every American believes in spite of the innumerable ways he fosters inequality in his support of the economic system, the political system, the educational system." The American identity is wrapped up in fraught issues, but still Americans move forward.

★ CHRONOLOGY ★

★ ★ ★ ★ ★ ★ ★

1491 More than fifty million people live in what will become the Americas; ten million of those people live in what will become the United States.

1607 Virginia becomes a colony.

1763 The Treaty of Paris ends the French and Indian War and launches the thirteen colonies' revolt against Great Britain.

1775 Thousands of individuals, carrying their own personal guns, arrive in Concord, Massachusetts, in time for what will become the first day of the Revolutionary War, April 19.

1783 The Treaty of Paris ends the Revolutionary War, establishes the borders of the United States, and recognizes American independence.

1787 Delegates to the Constitutional Convention in Philadelphia sign the Constitution.

1796 George Washington's farewell address says a lot about American and national identity.

★ ★ ★ ★ ★ ★ ★

★ ★ ★ ★ ★ ★ ★

1812–1815

The War of 1812 strengthens American identity.

1823 The Monroe Doctrine says that the United States will not become involved in European situations and will not tolerate European interference in its own.

1848 The Seneca Falls Convention in New York lays the groundwork for women being allowed to vote.

1861–1865

The Civil War divides the United States.

1865 The Thirteenth Amendment is added to the Constitution.

1866 The country's first civil rights bill, the Civil Rights Act, is passed in response to black codes.

1877 The Compromise of 1877 ends Reconstruction.

1887 The Dawes Act creates what are now known as Indian reservations.

1898 Puerto Rico becomes part of the United States.

1924 The Indian Citizenship Act expands US citizenship to all Native peoples.

1931 Congress names "The Star-Spangled Banner" as the United States' national anthem.

★ ★ ★ ★ ★ ★ ★

American and National Identity

★ ★ ★ ★ ★ ★ ★

1942 Executive Order 9066 forces thousands of issei, Japanese immigrants, and nisei, first-generation Americans born to parents who had immigrated from Japan, out of their homes and into camps.

1950s The Red Scare peaks.

1963 Dr. Martin Luther King Jr. delivers his "I Have a Dream" speech at the March on Washington.

1969 The Stonewall Riots take place.

2001 The September 11 attacks bring Americans together but also lead to a spike in hate crimes against Muslim-Americans.

2017 Puerto Ricans vote in favor of starting the process to become a state.

★ ★ ★ ★ ★ ★ ★

★ GLOSSARY ★

★ ★ ★ ★ ★ ★ ★

abolitionist Someone who opposes slavery.

Americanism Allegiance to the traditions, interests, or ideals of the United States; something particularly American.

Anglophobia Anti-British feelings or fears.

assimilation The process of being absorbed into the cultures, traditions, ways of life of another group.

Confederate Someone who sided with the South in the American Civil War.

Constitution of the United States The document that established the new country's government, its foundational laws, and its citizens' basic rights.

culture areas People with similar languages and ways of living, as identified by modern researchers.

Democratic-Republicans One of the first American political parties.

Era of Good Feelings A national mood that strengthened a unified identity, if only for a short time.

★ ★ ★ ★ ★ ★ ★

Federalist One of the first American political parties; members supported a strong federal government, including a national economy and justice system.

identity politics People grouping together based on common traits and for political reasons.

Loyalists People who sided with, or were loyal to, Great Britain during the American Revolution.

melting pot What the United States is often considered, because people of various background have come together under one set of national rules.

mercantilism A leading European economic practice in the 1500s through 1800s; it said countries should export more than they import and gather wealth in gold.

nationalist Someone who wants independence for a country.

Patriot In this book, someone who supported independence from Britain.

patriotism Love for or devotion to a country.

self-determination Independent freedom to decide one's future.

Union The North during the American Civil War.

Whigs A political party that advocated for a national bank and tariffs to benefit the United States.

★ ★ ★ ★ ★ ★ ★

Books

Chernow, Ron. *Alexander Hamilton*. New York: Penguin, 2005.

Kostyal, K. M. *The Founding Fathers: The Fight for Freedom and the Birth of American Liberty*. Washington, DC: National Geographic, 2016.

Shoup, Kate. *Peaceful Protesters: The Freedom Riders*. New York: Cavendish Square, 2018.

Websites

Define American

https://defineamerican.com

This nonprofit organization uses story, language, and media to create new definitions of identity, particularly around questions of "who is an immigrant?" and "who is an American?"

★ ★ ★ ★ ★ ★ ★

★ ★ ★ ★ ★ ★ ★ ★

We Are the Dream

https://getschooled.com/we-are-the-dream-us

This campaign, created by MTV and Get Schooled (which offers resources to help high school students succeed in the college preparation and application process), focuses on young people who are classified as undocumented—identified sometimes as American and sometimes as not.

Whose Heritage? Public Symbols of the Confederacy

https://www.splcenter.org/sites/default/
files/whoseheritage_splc.pdf

The Southern Poverty Law Center's 2015 report offers a map and chart of public Confederate imagery in the United States as well as a community action plan to remove those symbols of identity.

Videos

**Is It Healthy for America's Identity
to Keep Our Eyes Closed?**

https://www.tedmed.com/talks/show?id=7367

Bryan Stevenson, of the Equal Justice Initiative, speaks about the role of individual identities in shaping a bigger social identity.

★ ★ ★ ★ ★ ★ ★ ★

The Natives and the English - Crash Course US History #3

https://youtu.be/TTYOQ05oDOI

John Green provides a succinct summary of the interactions between Native Americans and early colonists, two groups with unique identities that helped form American identity as we know it today.

What Does My Headscarf Mean to You?

https://www.ted.com/talks/yassmin_abdel_magied_what_does_my_headscarf_mean_to_you/details

Yassmin Abdel-Magied, named Young Australian Muslim of the Year in 2007, speaks with humor and empathy about first impressions and supporting people of all identities.

★ ★ ★ ★ ★ ★ ★

★ BIBLIOGRAPHY ★

★ ★ ★ ★ ★ ★ ★

Ahlquist, Dale. "Lecture 37: What I Saw in America." The American Chesterton Society. Retrieved April 2, 2018. https://www.chesterton.org/lecture-37.

Avlon, John. "The Things George Washington Worried About Are Happening." History.com, February 16, 2018. https://www.history.com/news/washington-farewell-address.

Ayers, Edward L. "The Civil War, Emancipation, and Reconstruction on the World Stage." AP Central. Retrieved April 2, 2018. https://apcentral.collegeboard.org/series/america-on-the-world-stage/american-civil-war-emancipation-reconstruction-on-world-stage?course=ap-united-states-history.

Bear, Charla. "American Indian Boarding Schools Haunt Many." NPR, May 12, 2008. https://www.npr.org/templates/story/story.php?storyId=16516865.

Dropp, Kyle, and Brendan Nyhan. "Nearly Half of Americans Don't Know Puerto Ricans Are Fellow Citizens." *New York Times*, September 26, 2017. https://www.nytimes.

★ ★ ★ ★ ★ ★ ★

com/2017/09/26/upshot/nearly-half-of-americans-dont-know-people-in-puerto-ricoans-are-fellow-citizens. html?mcubz=1.

Encyclopedia Britannica. "Dawes General Allotment Act." Retrieved April 2, 2018. https://www.britannica.com/ topic/Dawes-General-Allotment-Act.

Ferling, John. "Myths of the American Revolution." *Smithsonian*, January 2010. https://www. smithsonianmag.com/history/myths-of-the-american-revolution-10941835.

Gibson, Carrie. "How Colonialism and Racism Explain the Inept US Response to Hurricane Maria." *Vox*, October 7, 2017. https://www.vox.com/the-big-idea/2017/10/5/16426082/colonialism-racism-american-response-puerto-rico-maria.

Goodridge, Elisabeth. "For Blacks, There Was No Clear Choice." *U.S. News & World Report*, June 27, 2008. https:// www.usnews.com/news/national/articles/2008/06/27/ for-blacks-there-was-no-clear-choice.

Hendrix, Steve. "The Day White Virginia Stopped Admiring Gen. Robert E. Lee and Started Worshiping Him." *Washington Post*, October 8, 2017. https://www. washingtonpost.com/news/retropolis/wp/2017/08/22/

the-day-white-virginia-stopped-admiring-gen-robert-e-lee-and-started-worshipping-him/?noredirect=on.

Hickey, Donald. "An American Perspective on the War of 1812." PBS. Retrieved April 2, 2018. http://www.pbs.org/wned/war-of-1812/essays/american-perspective.

Hindley, Meredith. "World War I Changed America and Transformed Its Role in International Relations." *Humanities*, Summer 2017. https://www.neh.gov/humanities/2017/summer/feature/world-war-i-changed-america-and-transformed-its-role-in-international-relations.

History.com. "18th and 21st Amendments." 2010. https://www.history.com/topics/18th-and-21st-amendments.

Indian Country Today. "The War of 1812 Could Have Been the War of Indian Independence." May 17, 2017. https://indiancountrymedianetwork.com/history/events/the-war-of-1812-could-have-been-the-war-of-indian-independence.

Jones, Robert P. "The Collapse of American Identity." *New York Times*, May 2, 2017. https://www.nytimes.com/2017/05/02/opinion/the-collapse-of-american-identity.html.

Juffer, Jane. "Reading, Writing, and Decolonization: Albizu Campos High School, a Controversial Alternative for Hispanic Youth." *Chicago Reader*, October 22, 1987. https://www.chicagoreader.com/chicago/reading-writing-and-decolonization-albizu-campos-high-school-a-controversial-alternative-for-hispanic-youth/Content?oid=871308

Kelly, Martin. "The Southern Colony." *ThoughtCo*. Last updated July 21, 2017. https://www.thoughtco.com/south-carolina-colony-103881.

King, Gilbert. "What Paul Robeson Said." *Smithsonian*, September 13, 2011. https://www.smithsonianmag.com/history/what-paul-robeson-said-77742433.

Landrieu, Mitch. "How I Learned About the 'Cult of the Lost Cause.'" *Smithsonian*, March 12, 2018. https://www.smithsonianmag.com/history/how-i-learned-about-cult-lost-cause-180968426.

Loewen, James W. *Lies My Teacher Told Me: Everything Your American History Textbook Got Wrong*. New York: Touchstone, 2007.

———. "Why Do People Believe Myths About the Confederacy? Because Our Textbooks and Monuments Are Wrong." *Washington Post*, July 1, 2015. https://www.washingtonpost.com/posteverything/wp/2015/07/01/

why-do-people-believe-myths-about-the-confederacy-because-our-textbooks-and-monuments-are-wrong.

Owen, Ken. "National Identity and the American Revolution." The Junto, December 27, 2012. https://earlyamericanists. com/2012/12/27/national-identity-and-the-american-revolution.

Pruitt, Sarah. "Uncovering the Secret Identity of Rosie the Riveter." History.com, January 23, 2018. https://www. history.com/news/rosie-the-riveter-inspiration.

Rigoglioso, Raymond L. "Stanford Scholar Tells History of Cold War from African American Perspective." *Stanford News*, March 8, 2017. https://news.stanford. edu/2017/03/08/cold-war-african-american-perspective.

Song, Sarah. "What Does It Mean to Be an American?" *Daedalus*, Spring 2009. https://www.amacad.org/ content/publications/pubContent.aspx?d=744.

Stokes, Bruce. "What It Takes to Truly Be 'One of Us.'" Pew Research Center, February 1, 2017. http://www. pewglobal.org/2017/02/01/what-it-takes-to-truly-be-one-of-us.

Toppo, Greg, and Paul Overberg. "After Nearly 100 Years, Great Migration Begins Reversal." *USA Today*, February 2, 2015. https://www.usatoday.com/story/

news/nation/2015/02/02/census-great-migration-reversal/21818127.

Vicens, AJ. "The Lost History of Puerto Rico's Independence Movement." *Mother Jones*, April 21, 2015. https://www.motherjones.com/media/2015/04/puerto-rico-independence-albizu-campos.

Wheelan, Joseph. "How the Civil War Changed America Forever." *Daily Beast*, April 8, 2015. https://www.thedailybeast.com/how-the-civil-war-changed-america-forever.

White, Richard. "The Rise of Industrial America, 1877–1900." The Gilder Lehrman Institute of American History. Retrieved April 2, 2018. https://www.gilderlehrman.org/history-now/rise-industrial-america-1877-1900.

Ydstie, John. "'1491' Explores the Americas Before Columbus." NPR, August 21, 2005. https://www.npr.org/2005/08/21/4805434/1491-explores-the-americas-before-columbus.

★ INDEX ★

★ ABOUT THE AUTHOR ★

★ ★ ★ ★ ★ ★ ★

Kristin Thiel lives in Portland, Oregon. She has written many books for Cavendish Square Publishing, on topics ranging from science and technology to history and current affairs. Her first book was a biography of Dorothy Hodgkin, a Nobel Prize–winning crystallographer. She is also the author of *Discovering America: Politics and Power in the United States*.

★ ★ ★ ★ ★ ★ ★

American and National Identity